Practical Solutions

for America

Robert West

In Memory of

Lt. John Calhoun

Commander Richard J. Hobbie

Lt. William Costen

Contents

Forward

When I began the Five Star Plan my target was career politicians from both sides. Specifically, the politicians who care more about the career than the people or the nation.

During this journey I have spoken to many politicians. Some have told me that solving an issue would cost them the support of the people pushing that issue. I have been told by Republican officials that the delegates to the GOP State Convention are merely activists with enough funds to attend and therefore do not "represent" the party.

Some conservative groups have blacklisted me because they have no interest in term limits or replacing bad politicians. Those politicians return their phone calls or speak at their meetings. Replacing all the bad ones would mean they would have to spend more time and energy to get to know all the new ones. I have seen Republican CEC's remove censures they passed from their websites under the threat of never having the elected attend their meetings. I have also seen the elected install paid staffers to party offices.

At times it has felt as if I have stumbled through the looking glass and wound up in an alternate world. But this is our world so the next question is "Am I crazy for trying?"

There are political organizations out there where the focus is how much attention they can get, how much money they can raise or how big they can grow their groups. Attempting to ally with such groups is almost impossible, they have their main objective and fixing the broken political system is something to be done after their main objective is reached. Never mind they have never actually established what that end goal might be.

I ran into GOP County Chairs across more than a dozen counties that REFUSED to seat volunteers for empty precinct chair positions. In some cases, they LOST the candidate applications for people seeking the office. These volunteers were found at conservative groups and gun shows; they are life-long Republican voters. The idea that the GOP did not wish to grow their numbers before an election was confusing to me.

In Smith County, Texas the GOP County Executive Committee voted on whether they would follow the state GOP list of legislative priorities. These priorities were passed in 2022 just 30 days prior; the vote was 17-14 to keep it. From a Republican governor that ordered churches closed in 2020 to a precinct chair that refused to say anything about it because Abbott was his boss, the entire chain is riddled with cowards and cronies.

There are good people holding offices, but they are so outnumbered and beat down it is depressing and they need reinforcements. Between the incumbent advantage, the ignorance of most voters and the GOP staying out of the Republican primaries, it is crucial that we start at the voting precinct to fix things. Once these precinct chairs are filled, we will have enough good people involved that we can work our way towards the governor's mansion. This is the only path I see that has any hope of reforming the government in every state & the nation.

I am not promising a quick or easy fix but I am promising this plan can and has worked when applied across the districts in question.

My background is aircraft electronics and there is a thing called "root cause analysis." If a light bulb burns out ten flights in a row you can keep replacing the bulb OR you can find out what is causing the bulb to burn out. We have problems and we must figure out what that "something" else is that is causing them.

At the beginning of the lock-downs in 2020 I sat down and thought about how we got to this place. How, in a conservative state like Texas, churches could be shut down, control of private business could be seized, courts closed and other such things could happen. What I came up with was career politicians. These people have spent their lives building a career in politics and who wants to switch careers? Many of these people decided on this career path while in high school and picked a college based on political science classes. Many of these people might have started out with pure intentions but they have become addicted to being in office. Addicts will do drastic things to feed their addiction and the results are what we are experiencing today.

A career politician in almost every case will switch political parties if it will help them reach their goal. They will violate their oath and abandon all integrity if it helps get them elected, re-elected or elected to the next higher office. Politicians who campaign for another job, while already holding an office are akin to salaried employees that instead of working, spend all day on interviews for a better job. The career becomes more important than the job, the state or the nation. This is not a party issue; this is a career politician issue.

If we can end politics as a career, we can save this nation. Elected office should be a service, much like jury duty. Anyone that wants on a particular jury should not be allowed anywhere near it. We need people willing to serve, not people desperate to win an office at any price.

I looked at political groups and found many of the same issues. Groups whose focus seemed to be raising funds, gaining recognition or growing but not interested in fixing the problems at all. Even officers inside the political parties are turning away volunteers and holding more than one office at a time instead of stepping aside to allow others the chance to serve. I am convinced that party officers, activist and yes, even political writers have a shelf life and should go away after a few years to allow others the chance to rise.

Many of these groups offer endorsements and have a vested interest in keeping their people in office for as long as possible. I followed suit my first year and endorsed some 40 people in 2021/2022. I will not be doing that again in 2024, why? In my home state of Texas there are 254 counties, over 50 congressional districts and more additional offices than I care to think about. There is no way I could possibly vet all these people and all their opponents. Then what happens if a better person steps up on the last day to register? It was a time sucking nightmare and I only had the word of these candidates to go by.

In 2024 I will endorse people I know and trust but as an individual, not as The Five Star Plan. If candidates like TFSP, then they can talk about it. Voters can ask candidates if they support TFSP and if you have read my first book then you know what questions to ask.

Too many voters are using endorsements as a crutch and not bothering to question the candidates on their own. It is really that hard to check your sample ballot before the election? Anyone can research for themselves and see who is saying what or find out who has voted the right way if you are leaning towards incumbents. Do not depend on the elected, the conservative groups or even the party to fix things, that is your job.

Imagine you get the voters list for your voting precinct. This is public information and, in many cases, it will cost nothing and can be received through an email. Now this list is all the registered voters broken down by name or address or if they voted in the last election. If you pull the information for just your political party you could decide to make 10 calls a week and recruit good people to help change things. This is something that I like to call, a precinct team. If you can get one person out of ten to help, at the end of the year you would have 53 people counting yourself. Fifty-two people probably does not sound like much but they could do the same the following year and you would have 2,704.

That amount of new people involved is often enough to decide county level elections. If those newly active people followed the example, it would become 273,104 and that could decide congressional or even state-wide elections. The next number is 14,201,408 and now we are talking about deciding who sits in the White House. This would take one person four years to accomplish but what kind of activity would make a greater impact than making those 10 calls a week?

Many of the victories we have had are credited to The Five Star Plan when we had nothing to do with them. While some of our greatest successes will never be known and that is okay. Imagine where we would be as a race if all the time and energy spent placing blame and claiming credit had been directed towards getting the job done. If you have not read my first book, read it and get the job done because we are running out of time.

1

The Middle

When I wrote the original Five Star Plan, I had the goal of getting Governor Greg Abbott censured across Texas by his own party for his violations of the Texas and US Constitutions. Fifteen county GOPs, including my own, did just that. A sitting governor has never had that happen to them in the history of Texas.

This effort was not enough to defeat him in the primary election and as I write this, he has just been sworn into office for a third term. Did I fail? I didn't get rid of Abbott and replace him with a good conservative. I did however, make a big difference in Texas politics that nobody would have thought possible given my lack of resources and history.

My wife and I seated or caused to be seated, several hundred new GOP precinct chairs. Other organizations and individuals using our template seated more. Even the GOP seemed to take a renewed interest in getting precinct chairs filled since TFSP came out. The Collin County GOP, once hopelessly establishment, has been entirely replaced. Members of a group called We the People, of Allen make up a huge percentage of those new precinct chairs. The Wise County GOP, top to bottom, has been replaced due to The Wise County Conservatives. Other counties across Texas have seen this and have taken the reins from the establishment and more will follow.

I have been interviewed by the University of Texas Horn and been on a couple of national shows but more surprising, I have sold copies of "The Five Star Plan" across the United States and been contacted by people as far away as England.

Out of the 40 or so candidates we endorsed, five won their elections but the rest are determined to try again or at the very least support someone as good as themselves next time around.

The power of the precinct chairs has been proven with the censure of State Representative Chris Paddie. Who, 30 days after declaring his bid for re-election withdrew his candidacy and then resigned from his office. Paddie did this after three of the six counties he represented censured him and the rest had begun the process.

I have lost track of the number of offices I have been asked to run for but for now, it seems I am doing more for the state of Texas than if I were in any office. I have often said, elected office should be treated like jury duty, not a career, but a duty. Anyone wanting to be on a particular jury should never be allowed anywhere near that jury box and anyone that wants an office should not be allowed near it. I am willing to serve in office, just like I am willing to serve on a jury, but so far, I have avoided both.

Romans 13 says we are to respect and obey our rulers, those placed in positions of authority by GOD, to do otherwise is to disrespect GOD. In the United States though, we are the rulers. GOD has put us in charge of this land and it is our servants that should read Romans 13. It is our public servants who should fear us and remember that GOD placed us in the position of authority, not the other way around. People that do not believe in GOD cannot believe in our system of government. If someone does not believe in GOD, they cannot logically believe in God-given rights.

We face a lot of issues and not the least of which is our loss of our culture. What is culture but a shared set of beliefs, customs and morality? More and more, we have no common set of beliefs and values and as those break down, we become weaker as a people. We also become more and more isolated and divided.

The very language is being rewritten in a bizarre fashion that not even George Orwell would have believed possible. At least in his book "1984" the government replaced definitions on a continuous basis. In our world the Supreme Court erased the meaning of "marriage" but offered no replacement. Nobody has an issue with defining what a "man" is but for some reason the definition of woman has been erased with no one offering a firm replacement.

Even the term "Democratic" as it relates to what that party was founded to promote is gone because when the Supreme Court returned abortion to the voters it made that part of law more "Democratic" but it was not greeted that way by the left in this country.

To be fair the word "Republican" would have made you believe those assuming that identity would support a limited, constitutional, republican form of government but many Republicans could not wait to vote for a man that has assumed "Emergency Powers," violated the constitution and has deprived Texans of a constitutional form of government for three years.

I recently read an article that stated only about 50% of those that attend church are registered to vote. Only about 50% of those, vote. Why is that? One reason is that we have heard "separation of church and state" so often we believe it to be true. What a great tool of dishonesty is for destroying nations and spreading misery.

I made sure both of my children read the United States Constitution several times while they were growing up. We talked about what they thought it meant, what I thought it meant and what other people thought it meant. When was the last time you read the "owner's manual" for our country? When was the last time you discussed it with your kids?

People that say they believe in our form of government, minus GOD, cannot believe in our form of government. You cannot believe in "GOD given rights" if you do not believe in GOD. Too many in the church believe the "Ten Commandments" were added to the Supreme Court building by mistake and too many do not see "In GOD we Trust" on our money. If religion and our government were separated then why use the bible to swear people into office? Why have invocations or be in the process of building The National Cathedral?

Since we are not a nation that separates our religion and our government then why have the faithful decided to leave voting to the unchurched by and large? Why surrender that power to those with less self-control and fewer morals?

For many people in the church, they see politics and politicians as tainted. They feel that the process and those involved have become so corrupt they no longer wish to be anywhere near it. Do these people think they will be worse off if they vote or pay attention? I can promise you the process and the politicians will not improve when our best citizens step away and abandon their power. We cannot surrender our voice to the unchurched, things will only get worse and despair is not the high moral road. Only one side in the Bible asks for you to despair, to spread defeatism and lies and it is not the side you want to be on.

Many Christians are simply tired of being made the fool and disappointed by people they thought were good. I get that, it has happened to me in almost every aspect of my life. Find people that are better and console yourself that you might have been right, they might have been good people when elected and then went bad. Politics is like peeling an onion, there are layers and most of them will make you cry so vote to replace them. Do not seek perfection on this side of paradise because it only leads to disappointment. Seek to find better people than the ones that hold the office now. Perfection is impossible, better should be a piece of cake.

Have you read this scripture from Romans 13: 1-5 or possibly heard it in a sermon?

Romans 13: 1-5

"Obey the rulers who have authority over you. Only God can give authority to anyone, and he puts these rulers in their places of power. 2 People who oppose the authorities are opposing what God has done, and they will be punished. 3 Rulers are a threat to evil people, not to good people. There is no need to be afraid of the authorities. Just do right, and they will praise you for it. 4 After all, they are God's servants, and it is their duty to help you. If you do something wrong, you ought to be afraid, because these rulers have the right to punish you. They are God's servants who punish criminals to show how angry God is. 5 But you should obey the rulers because you know it is the right thing to do, and not just because of God's anger."

In our system of a government of, by and for the people WE are the RULERS. Those public SERVANTS that we elect should fear and respect us. Read this passage more often; now reread it again with the sure knowledge our Founders set us apart as a nation of kings and queens who hired public SERVANTS to run the government. We are the rulers GOD has placed over the public SERVANTS, not the other way round.

Now, what does GOD expect from a ruler? Would HE want you to turn away from the responsibilities and gifts HE has bestowed upon us? Would HE want us to select evil servants who abuse their authority or leave them in that position for eternity?

Do not use Romans 13 to escape your duty, use it to define what that duty is and who you want as servants in public office. If you have a church, then certainly you have people that are more trustworthy than some of the public officials we have now. We need to get people with good hearts into those positions and rid our nation of the self- serving, career politicians.

When good people turn away from politics it only leaves one kind in charge and we do not want those people in charge of anything.

I have been told by many that it is too late to save this nation, that we are past the point of no return. I disagree with that 100%. If I am wrong, I have wasted some time, if they are wrong, they are wasting their chance.

2

Parties Do Not Believe

At the time of the founding of our nation there were people that were OK with a king, they even offered a crown to Washington who turned it down. There were huge fans of direct democracy but a majority felt that a direct democracy would be fickle and trample the rights of the minority. Our founders settled on a republican form of government where we would rule through our elected representatives.

The push and pull continues. Do we need more direct voting on issues pushing us towards a more democratic direction, or less direct voting which would be more, republican? The current problem we face, is that neither party seems to truly believe in what their titles would indicate. Governor Greg Abbott is a prime example. He has just been reelected governor of Texas and is still renewing his "emergency powers" in defiance of the Texas Constitution, Article 2, Separation of Powers. Since the first Covid lockdowns Texas has not had a limited, constitutional, republican form of government and the GOP voters seem fine with that.

Across Texas one might believe this country was founded upon one principle, "to beat the Democrats." The same could be true in your state. The very idea of replacing a tyrant or a bad incumbent in the primary or in the general is an alien concept. The majority of Texas Republicans are good with a king, if that king has an "R" by their name instead of a "D."

Recently, SCOTUS overturned Roe vs. Wade. This ruling returned the power to the states to decide an issue not addressed in the US Constitution. This ruling allows the people to vote on this issue but the Democratic Party did not like it. I thought that they believed more direct voting was better? Democrats certainly want gun rights to be decided by voters where such people agree with them, but not when it comes to abortion. Where Democrats do not overwhelmingly support more democracy, the Republicans overwhelmingly do not support a limited, constitutional, republican form of government.

I don't want to leave out the Libertarians from this discussion so allow me to turn to them for just a moment. "We believe there is too much top-down centralization of power in this country and things should be handled more at the local level." If you agree with us, send your donations to XYZ, Washington, D.C. headquarters. This reminds me of the Flat Earth Society webpage where they bragged about having members from around the world.

My wife, myself and about 5,000 other delegates participated in the 2022 Texas Republican convention. When Senator Cornyn took the stage, he was booed for 15 minutes. Afterwards he went back to DC and voted to spend more money to encourage states to adopt unconstitutional red flag laws. Eight GOP counties passed censure against him for this but the Texas SREC voted against the thousands of delegates and for the senator. You see, the state party does not believe you should censure a Republican during the election year or in a year leading up to an election year. Unfortunately, these are the only two types of years. The party leadership does not want you to censure a Republican before the primary, during the general or any other time. John Cornyn was not up for reelection, he sided with the Democrats on the red flag law and within a few days after our state convention. Yet the elites still sided with the incumbent over their party members.

So, what do the parties believe in? They believe that the longer a problem lasts, the better it is for them. If the other side can be blamed then the suffering will help them. If the problem causes pain to their supporters and they can convince those supporters they are working on it, then the campaign volunteers and donations will continue pouring in.

Democrats rail against Republicans trading stock while in office and Republicans rail against Democrats growing rich the same way. Why not unite and adopt party platform planks that result in anyone caught in this act loses the support of either party? The truth is that neither side has a problem with this practice, it is just a club to hit the other side with instead of fixing the problem. What is the stance of the elected? They passed a law that says the max penalty for anyone in Congress caught doing what is called "insider trading" is nothing more than a $200 fine instead of federal prison time. Is it any surprise that both Republicans and Democrats voted for this measure?

In 2020, I was involved with a congressional selection process and pointed out that the party platform calls for term limits. When I asked several conservative groups if they support "term limits" almost every hand in the room went up. When I promised to "term limit" myself to a max of two terms and to NEVER run for any other office there were only two reactions; an eye roll followed by "I have heard that before" and absolute fear followed by "but what if you are really, really good?" Surprise, when push comes to shove people believe in term limits for the other side, for people they do not like, not for everyone. Many of you, if you are still reading, are saying "So tell me something I don't know."

The fix is not complicated We need to replace party people that laugh and vote against us with people that will not. After that is done it is a simple matter to hold the elected accountable and to get rid of the ones that do not follow the will of the people.

Both parties believe in getting their person elected but both should be just as concerned with replacing bad members of their own parties in the primary election. Both parties offer the same solution to send emails, call and speak to your representatives. This is a waste of time because politicians know what you want, most simply do not care.

Matthew 7:18 "A good tree cannot bring forth evil fruit, neither can a corrupt tree bring forth good fruit."

It is not possible for a good tree to give bad fruit, and a bad tree will not give good fruit. Do you believe in the bible? How long will you shake a thorn tree and expect an apple to fall? How long will you beg and plead your representative to do the right thing? Good representatives do not have to be asked and bad representatives will not grant your wishes. Until and unless we rebuild these political parties with people more concerned with the future of this nation than the next gala and photo opportunity, we cannot even begin a mass replacement of bad incumbents.

How can we do this? What can one person do? I want to introduce you to a man named Andy Hopper from Wise County Texas, just North of Dallas. Andy formed a conservative group, not a "Republican" group. This group has arranged events of up to 200 people and brought in speakers such as Sid Miller, Chad Prather and others, including myself. When Mr. Hopper complained to me about his county GOP doing nothing, I asked, "How many precinct chairs are empty?" He responded with "All of them as far as I can tell." I then asked "You have 200 people attending your meetings, how many volunteers can you get to fill those empty seats?" He came back with, "We have asked but the County Chair does not hold meetings and refuses to fill them, what can we do?" was the reply.

I love that question and told him to, "get the list together and I will help you in any way that I can." It took a while but working together, mostly over the phone,

Andy managed to get a few select people at the state level to point out that turning away volunteers was not the best way to grow a party. He managed to get 15 seats filled. During the primary with the help of these new precinct chairs, they managed to get Mike Drury elected to replace the "do-nothing" County Chair they had prior. Mike Drury was a Five Star Candidate, one of the 40 or so I supported that year. Wise County has replaced their GOP with patriots and I am proud to know Andy Hopper and to congratulate him on that accomplishment. We do not always agree on everything but that did not stop us from working together to make Texas a better place.

Collin County did essentially the same thing. A group called "We the People of Allen" filled vacant precinct chairs a few at a time until they had the majority. Once it was clear they had that majority, they showed up to every meeting and voted as a group. The "old guard" including the County Chair, resigned. Their new CEC continues to find new people to fill empty precinct chairs. The last time I received an update from them they had over 79% of the positions filled where the "old guard" had held steady at 20% for years.

We have a dozen or so county GOPs in Texas that are solid. Before publishing this book, I started reaching out and using my podcast to help additional counties do what Wise, Collin and a few others have accomplished. This has not been easy, it will not gain you fame or fortune but like jury duty, it is my responsibility.

I have a hero down in Smith County, Bob Brewer who is finding people to fill empty precinct chairs that have sat vacant for years. He says I inspired him but he is doing all the work so if you bump into "Five Star Bob" while visiting Tyler tell him "Hello" for me. At the time of this writing Smith County is still a work in progress but it is only a matter of time before their CEC is filled with real conservatives.

I have worked with "Convention of States" and "Texit people" to convince them to fill empty chairs. We have gained precinct chair volunteers by renting booths at gun shows while also speaking across Texas. It is amazing how many groups that spend so much time helping and pleading with the GOP look surprised when they realize they can take control of their local party. Why waste time asking when that time could be better spent getting elected? Shouldn't you have a voice at the table?

Bexar County gained over 150 new precinct chairs because one person acted. Quite often all you must do is to ask people, so why were they still empty? They sat empty because the party does not ask. You might get messages requesting for you to vote and donate but how many times has anyone asked you to fill an empty office or run for office?

My website asks you to "DO SOMETHING," you can search until you are blue in the face but you will never see a "Donate" button. My message is not new, it is nothing I invented but it has been revived, organized, and put into play to the point that I am beginning to hear it echo. I heard "Replacing Politicians with Patriots" from the convention stage, I heard "paper ballots" and "voting precinct counts," from a state senator. Echoes and then action are what I am after.

The Republican Party of Texas is starting to fill precinct chairs when before they were filled by "the same people" for years. Even conservative groups are beginning to cooperate and train rather than just meet once a month. Many have also adopted our "Motivate, Educate, Activate" tag lines or things close to it. People ask me if seeing all these things upsets me, because they often do not comment or credit The Five Star Plan. Not at all, the message and the progress are the only goal I am after. I did not set this up to get rich or famous, I set it up to make things better and it seems all three goals are being met.

What is step one towards making your county GOP look more like the person in the mirror? First you will contact your County Chair. Most counties have one for each major party. Contact them and ask if they have any "empty precinct chair positions." Your voting precinct is on your voter's registration card and if your precinct is empty then volunteer to fill it. Often you can be sworn in at the next meeting. Since we just had a census, we have almost 3,000 more chairs sitting empty in Texas; these can be filled quickly. If your chair is filled, get in contact with that current precinct chair and volunteer to help them. It is a good idea to see if maybe they are one of the "good ones" before deciding to run against them.

How does this take over the county? It does not because your next step is to get the voter rolls. Do this by asking your County Clerk or Elections Administrators for the voting list from the last primary election for just your party. Armed with this information and with the list of precincts with no chairs you simply start calling and asking for them to volunteer. As soon as you have a volunteer for one precinct, you move to another.

Now if you can fill a third or more of these seats with fresh faces that still does not give you a majority, does it? No, but you now have people at the meeting and they can tell you who needs to be replaced. Find people to run against the bad ones using the same method that helped you find volunteers to fill the empty seats. You now have these precinct chairs to help with the task. It is pretty much a coin toss as to who will win a precinct chair election but often, the challenger has the advantage. Once your county has 66/33 patriots verses the establishment the patriots have control. Expect several of the "do nothing" types to resign and then fill them with volunteers as fast as you can.

Why are so many seats empty? Glad you asked. Recall back to, "what parties do not really believe" what their names would indicate. The same applies to what they say in many cases. They will talk about "growing the party" but what they mean is getting more people to volunteer, vote and donate. Growing the actual number of people in the party dilutes their importance, influence, and control.

Mr. Big and Mr. Tall can bully four or five elderly precinct chairs to get his way, but can he do that with 30 or 40 patriots? Probably not. They will rationalize not seating fresh faces by saying, "the more chairs we have, the higher the chance of not reaching quorum." Remember that when some people rationalize, they end up just telling rational lies. The truth is that a decent precinct chair, knocking doors and making calls can increase voter turnout by 20 to 30 percent or more. In some cases, active precinct chairs will get turnouts well above the national average and become the point of contact for voters deciding on how to vote.

This is when it no longer becomes about beating the Democrat or beating the Republican. It becomes about electing the best person for the job and the one who truly believes in a republican form of government.

Take Action

Step 1 – Contact your County Chair and ask if they have open Precinct Chair positions. Their contact information can be found on the state party website menu.

Before contacting check your voters registration card for your precinct number. The goal is to find out if your PC position is filled or vacant. If occupied get that chair's contact information, otherwise request to fill the empty seat.

County Party______________________________________
County Chair______________________________________
Email/Phone______________________________________
Your Precinct #______________________________________
Precinct Chair______________________________________
PC Email/Phone______________________________________

Step 2 Get the Voter's list from the last primary election for your party. This can be acquired through your County Clerk or Elections Administrator.

Step 3 Use the voter information to create a precinct call list to find more people. These volunteers can help achieve the goal of filling empty precinct chairs in your county and activate voters towards increasing turnout for every election. This is also where you will find candidates for local and state offices.

Additional Notes

____

____

____

____

____

____

____

____

____

____

____

____

____

____

____

____

____

3

Real People Representing Us

Government of, for and by, the People. Our Founders set up a nation of kings and queens that hired public SERVANTS to run the government while we went about our lives. Too many people have forgotten who the "public" is and who the "servants" are on both sides of that equation. Servants do not tell you what to do, rather the other way around.

Our Founders envisioned that we would take turns at this "public servant" thing from time to time and then go back and lead our lives. The original constitution of Texas did not allow back-to-back public offices to be held. The reason Sam Houston was the 1st and 3rd President of Texas was not because he lost the second election, it was because the law did not allow him to serve terms back-to-back. This eliminated the "incumbent advantage" and all but guaranteed that there would be no career politicians. Every elected position was an open race.

The number of times I have heard career politicians justify not doing the right thing so that they could get reelected is staggering. If someone is more concerned with reelection than accomplishing anything, they need to never be in office.

Elected office and jury duty should be treated the same, something you are willing to do but not something you should never make a lifelong career. Can you imagine a jury member telling you they could not vote to convict someone they knew was guilty, because they want to get selected for jury duty again in the future? We have reached a point where a lotto system would give us better representation in DC and the state capitals. If we randomly selected our President, Senate and Congress with a drawing, tell me, "Would we not be better off than our current batch?" Since that is not going to happen, we all need to step up and run for public office or find regular people to run. The first step in getting rid of career politicians is finding good people to run against them.

Most states have political parties that can determine who they run in elections. When was the last time your state party turned away a bad candidate or told anyone that "This candidate of ours is bad and nobody should vote for him/her?" If your state political party refuses to hold their elected accountable then that party needs to be replaced. In aviation we often said, "You cannot do anything until you do something else first." It is the same in politics.

Across the country there are hundreds, if not thousands of political organizations and groups. Many are good and have a record of accomplishing a lot to make this nation better. Others are just money grabs and attention getters for their founders. One way to tell if a group is built for good instead of the cash and attention is if the leaders have chosen their replacements and have plans to turn over the organization in the future. Or do they want to be "dictator for life" over what they established? Often a person who refuses to even consider releasing the reins of power does not deserve the "tator" be added to their description.

The elected, the political organizations, parties and political groups can all be good or bad. Use discernment and compare what they have done over what they say they will do before supporting them. When in doubt, avoid them. There is nothing stopping you from building your own team and training your own replacement to avoid that trap.

Alright, so you have become a precinct chair or have found enough volunteers to be elected to hold the majority at the county level, now what? Step one is to announce this with a press release, step two is to contact your representatives to inform them of something they do not know. Namely, you will be telling your congressperson, state representative and state senator that you fully intend to pass "censure" against anyone voting against the party platform or openly advocating against the party platform planks. If the elected do not believe as the party believes then they will be replaced with someone who does.

Censure is merely calling "foul" on your teammates. The voters do not have to see the foul on their own, if their own team is telling you about it, it must be true. In many states a censure can result in getting kicked out of the party and not having your name on the ballot. When is the last time David Duke was allowed to run for office? The argument against "censure" is that it will help the "other" side win but the "other" side is already not voting for your candidate, the other side is also not running against them in the primary elections. If the other side isn't voting for your candidate, you have to ask why.

District-wide censure does work, Cass, Harrison and Shelby Counties proved that when they censured State Representative, Chris Paddie who not only pulled his name out of the reelection hat but resigned rather than be censured in the other three counties he supposedly represented. Another example is Joe Straus who was Speaker of the House in Texas, arguably the second most powerful position in Texas with Lt. Governor holding the most power. If it can work against that guy, it can work against anyone, it just involves people doing the work.

You also need to organize and select great people to run your state party. These people need to agree with fixing the problem and replacing the bad apples. They cannot be focused on building their own political futures. They need to be more about doing the right thing than getting reelected. It is not difficult to find these people so look to your newest members or those warhorses that have done the right thing on a consistent basis.

The rules and platform for your state party is often decided well before the state convention but if you have the right delegates then you can improve things. You can make it harder for bad apples to get away without punishment and set guidelines that push even the bad actors into at least pretending to be good to keep their jobs. This requires a lot of work and coordination because there are lots of tricks and traps that the people running these conventions can use to determine the outcomes such as burning a whole day on silly issues and then passing "everything else" in a single vote so you can get out of the building on time. They always seem to have time for a slate of speakers but never enough time to debate the rules and platform of the party, odd, right?

Once you gain control of your political party at the precinct level, county and then state you work to rewrite the rules and platform by making it easier to hold the elected accountable. In essence, you use the party to replace career politicians with patriots.

Congratulations, your state is in good shape, now share that with other people in other states and this nation will be on the right track again. The key to keeping it on the right track is the old adage, "Politicians are like diapers, they should be changed often, and for the same reason." This applies also to party office holders and political activists in general. It is far too easy to get hung up on keeping or gaining a position rather than the main goal, making things better. As soon as you get a position, start looking for your replacement. This is something I learned in the military and carried throughout my corporate years. I ended up being the "former boss" to the heads of many other departments. My bosses complained about my turnover but always asked me for favors when they needed one because many of those former subordinates still felt they owed me for helping them with their careers. They were glad to assist me with whatever I asked of them.

When I say that the people are in charge I mean it, even the people I don't agree with on a regular basis. I am not saying to cooperate with satanists or socialist but people that might support Texas Independence, by and large are asking for a vote on that topic. I can support them getting a vote, even if I plan on speaking and voting against the idea. I would rather have a Texit person in an elected position than a career politician. While I can disagree with their movement, I can bet that on just about every other topic, they will vote better than the career politician.

I can help the Convention of States people and get some of them elected. Until we replace the politicians that ignore our constitution, changing the constitution is pointless but having people that are passionate and agree with me on every other topic is worth the effort. This might get me banned from speaking to certain groups but I can even support some Democrats over certain Republicans. I have never met a Democrat that just wants to pave the left-hand side of the road, just as I have never met a Republican that just wants to pave the right-hand side of the road.

In fact, voting for a Democrat to get rid of a bad Republican is not unheard of in Texas and that could also be true in other states. I know of many Texas conservatives that voted for Senator John Cornyn's opponent in 2020 with the idea to vote him out of office since the party seems unwilling to do it for us.

The long and short of this chapter is that the founders would be disappointed in Americans if they heard us ask, "Who is in charge of the House or the Senate" or "which party won the White House" after an election. To them "the people" were always in charge; that was the whole point of the revolution and the constitution. Countless people have died protecting this country and I knew some of them. Determine how much time and effort you are willing to spare for the future of this country. Then put that time into action, not with me, but with your fellow citizens.

You do not have to agree with me on everything to get my help. If you want some common sense injected into government and if you want the elected to listen to the people instead of lording over us then we should talk. If you want the constitution followed instead of being ignored or violated then you are on my side. We do not have to share the same tax or defense positions and I am not concerned with how conservative you may or may not be. There are plenty of Democrats that support "freedom of speech" and the rest of your rights, including that 2nd amendment. There are plenty of Republicans that have violated those rights and voted against that 2nd one. It is easy to believe that voting straight party makes you a great citizen but until or unless you know the voting records of the elected, you could easily vote yourself into slavery by blindly supporting a party as easily as blindly supporting an individual. Stop trusting others and start trusting yourself, it should be easier, you know yourself better than you know them.

Take Action

Step 1 Once you have taken over your precinct, county and state party send out a press release for each success. Make this a public announcement in print, through a newsletter and via social media.

Local Newspaper_______________________________________

Contact Person_______________________________________

Phone/Email_______________________________________

County Newspaper _______________________________________

Contact Person_______________________________________

Phone/Email _______________________________________

Statewide Newspaper _______________________________________

Contact Person_______________________________________

Phone/Email _______________________________________

Step 2 Contact your elected representatives from state to federal. This information can be found on the secretary of state website. Most organized counties will have their elected representatives posted on their websites.

Reach out to inform them that you fully intend to pass a formal "censure" against anyone voting against the state and federal constitutions, the party platform or openly advocating against the party platform planks.

House District #________________________________
State Representative ____________________________
Contact Information_____________________________

Senate District#________________________________
State Senator __________________________________
Contact Information_____________________________

Congressional District#_________________________
Congressman___________________________________
Contact Information_____________________________

Senator ______________________________________
Contact Information_____________________________
Senator ______________________________________
Contact Information_____________________________

Additional Notes

4

Illegal Immigration

It might shock a few people to know I did not support the Trump wall. We have almost two thousand miles of southern border with about 700 miles of that being in Texas. To build such a wall would require that some property owners see their lands divided. The cost as with any government project is beyond the imagination of most people. At the time it was proposed I said you might as well build it with hundred-dollar bills as it will be worthless if the next administration orders the gates to be opened. You can Google "INS opens the gates," click "video" and watch it happen. What good does a wall do if the gates are ordered open?

We are financially broke as a nation; we borrow so much money it boggles the mind that anyone would still lend to us. So instead of building a wall, why not use what we already have, like the Social Security Administration.

Hiring someone that is an illegal gets you a fine but hiring someone without a social security card will put you in prison. Illegal aliens do not have valid cards, so how do they get jobs? That is easy, they use someone else's number. If you gathered a list of people from the SSA holding more than three full-time jobs in more than three states, at the same time, what are the odds that all the people associated with that one person's social security number are that one person?

Finding the illegals that arrived here after the wall was built is not difficult, we already have that information at our fingertips. Armed with those details we could round up all 15,738 Juan Valdez's using the same social security number and apologize to the one that is here legally. The rest should be charge with tax fraud, mail fraud, identity theft, illegal entry and probably a dozen other laws that they have violated including anything at all having to do with the IRS. Give them a choice between being sent to federal prison for the maximum sentence on each charge, served one after the other and deportation when finished or leaving on their own. The second choice would be they can plead guilty, pay a few thousand in fines, leave the USA and never return or else they have to serve that sentence. I am even willing to give them 90 days or so to get their affairs in order. The point is that it costs very little or even turns a profit. As word gets around others will leave before it happens to them. It would also deter people that wish to come here illegally better than a wall with an open gate.

Why has this not happened? Because Democratic leadership in DC want millions of new voters and they will try to find these illegals a "pathway to citizenship" so that they can get these votes. Republicans in DC like these illegals because it is cheap labor for some of their largest donors. They also help flood the SSA with dollars that they never have to pay back. It does not matter how many thousands of people pay into Mr. Valdez's account on that one SS number, only one check goes out when it is time for him to retire. Over the years both parties have robbed the SS "trust fund" so much that they need this accounting trick to cover their tracks for a few more years.

Short of a federal solution such as the one I just proposed, the states could solve this problem by declaring an invasion and repelling it. The US Constitution allows the states to defend themselves from "invasion" if the federal government fails to protect us. Otherwise, states would not have agreed to the constitution in the first place.

From the time Biden was declared the winner until this writing, an estimated five million illegals have crossed the borders of the United States. These illegals are coming from more than 180 countries around the world and arriving mostly through Texas. Based on the number of known terrorists apprehended and the estimated percentage of "got aways" it is no doubt an "invasion" with numbers each month climbing to almost twice as many people as participated in the Normandy Invasion. Not only have armed cartel members crossed the border and shot at our people, tens of thousands across the nation have died due to fentanyl. These deaths are not just drug users but innocent bystanders exposed by accident. People will continue dying of this "weapon" unless and until our government fulfills its duty to protect our border and our rights, including the right to life.

Murder, rape and robbery are at higher rates than they would be without massive illegal immigration and the next heartless SOB that touts that illegals are "less likely" to commit crime than the general population should know, we do not care. One additional murder, rape or robbery is way too many so they can feel superior as they defend five million criminals whose very first act upon arriving was to violate our immigration law, trespass on private lands and take our tax money away through enforcement, processing, transportation and assistance programs. If even 1% are actual criminals you have just condemned 50,000 people to be victims and that is if the criminals are caught on their very first crime. Notice these cowards that defend additional rapes, murders and robberies do not tend to live anywhere near a border but in nice safe gated communities.

Even the nut jobs in Seattle that declared themselves independent of the United States during 2020 put a wall around their "country" on the first day. None of these fools were Trump supporters so the wall idea was non-partisan.

Again, the solution is at the precinct, county, state and then the national level. Border states should declare an "invasion" and join with other states to declare a "compact" and activate the National Guard along with any volunteers that want to serve in the effort. Immediately return the invaders to the country they used to enter the USA and have a way to identify repeat offenders with a database. First action is to return, jail and then double the penalty for each additional return. Anyone attacking or firing at the guard will receive return fire, if they don't like that, then they can stop shooting at us first.

The states can solve this issue but it will not be cheap and unless or until we can get decent people elected to state positions it will not happen. Most careerist will gladly see you and your family raped and killed so long as their careers remain intact. Most career politicians care more about what the establishment thinks of them than a few voters. Secure borders are an issue with overwhelming support in the black and Hispanic communities with 25% of black Americans saying they have personally lost a job or contract to either an illegal or those employing illegals.

If the Republican Party wanted to expand their base this would do it in those two communities. The truth is that the Republicans and Democrats like having things close, so they can blame each other and keep voters divided, voting for each progressively worse candidate on both sides in order to "beat" the other. The reality is when both sides vote for worse and worse candidates in order to beat the other side, we all lose.

What to do? Get your county, then your state party to declare an invasion. Put anyone running for any county, state or federal office on the spot and have them publicly declare an "invasion" to even be considered. Eventually you will have enough people on record to get it done at the state level and it will spread.

At the federal level we must declare that the US Constitution applies ONLY to United State citizens as it clearly states. Also include that the birthright citizenship was "created" in the 1960's and must be clearly returned to those born to citizen parents.

Furthermore, there should not be a single cent spent on illegal aliens outside of incarceration, processing and their return. NO social security, NO private/public housing or assistance of any kind on the USA taxpayer and NO payment to non-Governmental organizations to care for them.

Take Action

Step 1 Get County elected officials to declare an invasion and then do the same push for your state elected officials.

To make this request at the county, attend commissioners court and speak in an open forum to share your request. You can also reach out prior to see if it can be added to their agenda for an open discussion and voted on at the next commissioner's court.

Once you get the county onboard reach out to your state representatives and ask for them to do the same. Insist on a follow-up to see if they even made the effort. I would recommend doing this in person at their local office. Most state senators and reps have an office near you.

County _______________________________
County Judge___________________________
Commissioner Court Date ________________

State Representative ____________________
Office Address__________________________
Phone_________________________________

State Senator___________________________
Office Address__________________________
Phone_________________________________

Step 2 For candidates running for state or federal office ask them to consider declaring an invasion as part of their platform.

Additional Notes

____
____
____
____
____
____
____
____
____
____

5

Voter Fraud

First and foremost, we are not reversing, redoing, or invalidating the 2020 election. Even if we could, it would be a nightmare that would cost far more than it gained us. Democrats were "election deniers" in 2008 and 2016. There was nothing wrong with that as far as they were concerned until Republicans questioned the results in 2020. Democrats saw nothing wrong with Biden comparing and asking for voter ID to "Jim Crow" on steroids.

All of that aside, can we all agree that faith in the elections is a requirement to avoid political violence in the future? Can we agree that BOTH sides have cheated in elections at some time in the past and that is also wrong?

How do we return faith in our elections? The first step is to end black box voting. If a machine is programmed, they can be programmed wrong. Your calculator can just as easily be programmed to tell you 2+2=6 as it can be set to tell you it equals 4. Can we all agree that if voting machines are NEVER connected to the internet, then they should not have modems which ONLY serve to connect machines to the internet?

Here is my solution. Each state adopts a system where you vote in person, with a valid ID in your voting precinct. The votes are tallied in each precinct when the polls close. The results are posted online that night with a representative from each party being present. These ballots are watermarked, serialized and hand marked. Then the results of each precinct are added up as they come in and posted at the county level. The county results are then totaled as they arrive and posted at the state level. This can be done with optical readers.

Yes, we can still have mail in ballots for military serving out of state, or the infirmed that cannot get to the polls. If we need more people to run the election, we can use the jury pool. I would also suggest filming the entire process and live streaming it for the world to see. From the first vote entered until the results are announced there is nothing wrong with filming this process and having it on the internet for a few weeks to avoid the appearance of fraud.

Before the results are reported the TOTAL NUMBER OF VOTES CAST will have already been announced at the local level of government. I have worked elections; the precincts know to the person how many people voted. If you "find" more votes than you had voters, it is fraud no matter who "finds" them.

I would insist that the penalty for voter fraud be raised to a felony and that no plea bargain can be made, ever. Presently if you get caught committing voter fraud, many states treat it as a misdemeanor; this includes Texas. The payoff for cheating is great, the risk is low and if you can get your side to win it is even lower.

The Constitution gives legislators the sole authority for determining the time, place and manner of our elections. If anyone changes those other than the legislators then the entire state loses its vote. If you do not want that to happen then it's simple, don't violate the constitution. For those of you that think I am talking about the five states that did this when Biden won, I am also talking about Texas where Greg Abbott decided to extend early voting because "The Emergency Powers Act" made him a dictator and yes, I added "tator" to be polite. For a list of the constitutional violations by Greg

Abbott, you can get them in my first book. As of this writing I also have the additional violations listed, making a total of 17, they can be found on my website in resources.

In many states the county can determine if they use paper or machines to conduct the elections. Your first step is to get people elected at that level to return us to an "unhackable" paper ballot system. Each precinct is relatively small so hand counting at the precinct level should be faster than what we are seeing now with the machines.

Next up is to clean the voter rolls. There are perhaps 10% fraudulent voters listed in the rolls. Getting married has created duplicate voters and it takes time to get them removed. College kids may also be registered in more than one county. I know for a fact that "Misti" and "Misty" who are both registered in Harrison County, TX at the same address and share the same last name are not, in fact, two different people. I know that there are not 80 something voters living at a certain street address on Tiger Lane in Harrison County, TX because that is the student center, not a dorm. Nobody lives there.

You can take the voters list provided by your County Clerk or Elections Administrator and sort it by address to see if an odd number of people live at any one address.

You can check your address and those of your friends and family to see if they have any additional voters at their houses. You can sort by names and see how many "Carri Annes Jean-Hathaway's" live at multiple addresses and are registered to vote at these several addresses. Hint, there is only one and being registered to vote and voting at all three addresses just might be voter fraud.

If you live in Smith County, Texas and are wondering why every tax increase seems to happen with 54% of the vote when 80% of the people say they voted against it there is a way you can determine that as well. Ask for the precinct vote totals. By Texas law they are public information as soon as the elections are finalized. Even asking for this information can be informative. People that think the elections are on the up and up will hand them right over, people that know the machines did not work but the elections were certified anyway might drag their feet. Make a note of it for later if you must file a FIA, Freedom of Information Act for something that belongs to you, the public.

Find the smallest precinct vote total. Say for example only 124 people voted in a certain precinct. You can get the voters list and see how many people voted in that precinct. Now just start calling them and ask each one straight up if they voted for or against the measure to verify the election results.

If you find that 75-80% voted "nay" but the results said 54% voted "yes" there is an issue, right? So, get 124 affidavits printed, grab a volunteer with a Notary Public Stamp and get those voters to sign those affidavits. Then turn them over to the DA for investigation, hold a press conference and keep copies just in case they get lost, because this does happen. Once you have proof that the election was a fraud as far as that precinct is concerned you can ask the county/state/feds to get involved. Fraudulent elections can certainly be treated as civil rights violations, at least they have been in the past. It does no good to allow everyone to vote if those votes are not counted correctly now does it?

Now for example, if this sort of thing should happen in Smith County, Texas or any other county it is reasonable to assume somebody or several somebodies were involved. At the very least those people should be stripped of any public office from now on.

Everyone should be reminded how they treated the voters and the veterans that fought for those voting rights in any future election they try to participate in. Again, this is just a hypothetical but a good example on how to act on suspicious election results. Keep in mind that although the career politicians have reduced voter fraud from a felony to a misdemeanor, conspiracy is still a felony.

Step 1 Get the voters rolls from your local government and go over them by precinct. Look for duplicate and multiple names at one address. Then take any suspicious finding to your voter's administration office so they can be corrected.

County_______________________________________
County Clerk Office___________________________
Voter Administration Office ___________________

Step 2 Bring the results to your Commissioner's Court and request paper ballots. If you want this to be open for discussion you must fill out a request to be added on their agenda prior to their scheduled meeting.

County Judge_________________________________
Judge Secretary ______________________________
Commissioner's Court_________________________

Step 3 Take things to the next level and put together a proposal of your own or the ideas I shared. Hand this off to your state representatives in person at one of their local office locations.
House Representative _________________________
Office Address_______________________________
Phone_______________________________________

State Senator _______________________________

Office Address_______________________________

Phone_______________________________

Additional Notes

____

____

____

____

____

____

____

____

____

____

____

____

____

____

____

____

____

____

____

____

6

Inflation

Inflation in a single product or several products can be caused by a variety of issues. General inflation, across an economy has only ever been caused by one thing, government policy. If you have any example of that not being the case, please clue me in. Anyone saying differently should be able to rattle off the one or more exceptions they think they may have. Be VERY suspicious if this current round of inflation is the only example in history where this is not the case.

You do not need a degree in economics to know that printing more money makes the money already in existence worth less. Money is the score for how much wealth is produced. If we can create more wealth, we can add an equal amount to the money supply and the money will be worth the same. If we create more wealth than we have money the cash becomes more valuable, if we just print money without creating wealth then the cash becomes worth less, in extreme cases worthless.

Google "hyperinflation" and look at the photos, read the stories, it is always the same story. Governments tried to print their way into prosperity instead of adding more actual value to the economy and the results were bad. If printing money worked, everyone would do it. If adding money to the system was such a great thing, counterfeiting would not be illegal.

I like to be honest so here is the truth. President Trump started this excess spending by passing out Covid relief checks that we could not afford. Biden did the same thing, only more so.

For people that have read the liberals view that "greedy corporations" are to blame, ask yourself, why did the corporations only learn to be greedy AFTER Biden spent over two Trillion dollars we did not have? Ask those same people to explain, when did the corporations become greedy for the very first time?

For the people that claim inflation to be a "world-wide" issue they are mostly correct, since the whole world seems to be taking the same approach. Here is the list of countries from Trading Economics with the lowest inflation numbers as of May 2022.

Countries with Lowest Inflation Numbers:
1. Hong Kong 1.2%
2. Bolivia 1.41%
3. Seychelles 2.1%
4. China 2.1%
5. Saudi Arabia 2.2%

Saudi Arabia has oil exports to help them avoid inflation. Meanwhile the United States has approved more regulations and roadblocks for oil exploration, development and transportation. This began in the very beginning of the Biden administration. Biden promised to "end the petroleum industry" even before being sworn into office. He also did this in the last presidential debate before the election. "Would you close down the oil industry?" President Donald Trump pressed just before their closing statements. "I would transition from the oil industry, yes" Biden replied.

These other nations simply did not print more money than their economies produced in wealth. To explain this to others you can use something as simple as the comic, Superman #1. This comic recently sold at auction for over $2 million. The company could, in theory, make perfect replicas of that comic. They own the rights, they know what ink, paper and staples to use. Now imagine if they did that and gave every American or even the world this perfect replica; this copy was so good nobody could tell the difference. Would we all have something worth $2 million or would the person with the original suddenly find his comic was worth less?

You might have seen a western movie where a guy walks into a story and buys a Henry rifle for a $20 gold piece. You can still get a great rifle for about an ounce of gold but that rifle or that gold would cost a lot more than $20. It is not that these things are any more valuable, it is simple that inflation has made the dollar worth less.

When the government prints money in excess of what value we have in our economy the money you have saved becomes worth less. This becomes a form of taxation. The total wealth of the nation is divided equally between all the dollars, even the bogus funds the government prints up which means your share is stolen.

How do we "fix" inflation? We must produce more goods and services in relation to the amount of money that is floating around. Historically interest rates must be adjusted about three points higher than inflation to bring it under control in the short term and that "solution" leads to a recession. Why recession, because people decrease spending and stop buying houses and cars as much because the interest rates are high. It takes a while and there is no way to "fix" it. Anyone, from either party that tells you otherwise is a liar.

You can inform your representative in Congress and the Senate that voting for ever increasing spending is a dealbreaker for you, even if it means staying home or voting for the other side. It really does not matter which party drives us over the cliff, both are headed in the same direction at only slightly different speeds.

Ask people this, "Would you be willing to cut your favorite government program if it meant no more federal income tax, ever?" Now cutting 10% across the board would not lead to this but if everyone could agree to cut their favorite program it would be. At the very least, we could get spending down to the point where someone could at least imagine a time when the debt could be paid off and all that interest could go to something besides renting money.

Take Action

Step 1 Remind your representatives in DC that voting to increase spending is a dealbreaker. Research your elected online through a statewide government website. For Texans you also can find your elected on TFSP website under Resources.

District____

Congress ____

Email/Phone _______________________________________

DC Senators____

Email/Phone____

Step 2 Track their voting record; if their records reflect over spending on more than three counts get your County Executive Committee to hold a vote for censure.

Additional Notes

____

____

____

____

____

____

____

____

____

____

____

____

____

7

They Don't Listen

How many times have you been told to write or call your elected representatives? Do you really think they don't know what you want? Do you really believe they care if a couple of thousand people call or show up at the capital? Sometimes it might have an impact, but there was a recent study that covers decades from both parties, concluding it to be a waste of time.

According to a recent study, what does matter is how much money you have. Martin Gilens of Princeton and Benjamin Page of Northwestern conducted a study that tracked about 2,000 issues from 1981 to 2002. This is a span of time where both Republicans and Democrats held power at various times.

Now one would think issues with 100% support would pass at a higher rate than an issue with 50% support and much more often than an issue with 0% support. This would be a sign of a well-functioning representative government. What they found surprised them. Only 30%. You might be asking if that is the percentage of issues that passed with 100%, 50% or 0% of public support. The answer is yes, 30% of the 2,000 issues passed and it did not matter what the general public thought of it. Now if you were to break down what the top 10% of income earners thought, well the system seems to work very well. What these people liked or did not like matched what laws passed or failed in excess of 90%.

Only about 1 in 200 people donate more than $200 a year to politicians. Those people really matter, the rest of us? Not so much. If something passed that you liked it was not because of that phone call you made, it was because the rich agreed with you. Even lobbyists do not have as good a track record as the elites. The general population's opinion matched the pass/fail rate 3% of the time. Special interest groups matched about half the time. What about the rich? They tracked about 76% of the time but the very rich tracked about 90% of the time.

Every hear of this Bible quote? "**A good tree cannot produce bad fruit**, nor can a bad tree produce good fruit…" Mathew 7:18

How much time have you and I spent trying to get bad people to do the right thing? How many times have we shown up, written or called out the elected only to have the exact opposite happen as what we wanted? I will no longer waste my time shaking a thorn tree attempting to get fruit. Instead, spend that time talking to people directly. Find and support good people to take the place of the bad ones.

It took Texas Republicans 20 years of state control to get permitless carry. The largest amount of pressure ever exerted in Texas politics was an attempt to get legislation passed to protect minors from gender modification and we got nothing. This was outlawed in Britain, so my next question is an easy one, "When did Texas become less conservative than Britain?"

The long and short is that the politicians know what we want, they simply do not care. This is not just a Republican or Democratic issue. Black Democrats want the border closed more than any other group in the United States and their politicians do not listen.

How do we solve this? By and large a politician must run as a Democrat or a Republican. If the parties were to gain control by good people, then both organizations could stop allowing bad people access to get elected. Freedom of association is still a thing in this country and no law can force a private group to allow others to use their brand.

The reason the two parties do not do this more often is that they are every bit as corrupt as the people they support. An incumbent has a huge advantage in elections. Both parties have seemingly forgotten that making the country better and having the will of the people obeyed by our public servants is the place to start. Both parties seem only interested in winning at any cost so it makes sense they would stay out of primaries or worse, openly support the incumbents. This needs to change.

The best course of action to improve this is by joining your local political party and fight to strip people from ever holding office that do not listen to their voters. Even if this means the other side wins an election. This is a better path than allowing our public servant to become our public masters.

If the political parties attempt to frighten you with what "the state," i.e., what "the elected" demand, then remind them you are not required to support them if they refuse to support you. There is no state law that says we must support bad people running for office.

Take Action

Step 1 Good people must lead our political parties. First find out if you have a precinct chair, if empty ask the county chair to be seated. If you have a do-nothing precinct chair then run against them in the primary.

County Chair_______________________________________

Email/Phone_______________________________________

Your Precinct_______________________________________
Precinct Chair _____________________________________
Email/Phone_______________________________________

Step 2 Join your local political party and offer to help fill empty precincts. Offer to establish precinct teams to grow the party and find good candidates.

Next Meeting_______________________________________

Step 3 Repeat this activity in surrounding counties by finding one or two people to mentor. Select counties that share the same senate and house district for state and federal offices. Many will overlap so you can multitask these efforts.

County_______________________________________
Name_______________________________________
Phone/Email_______________________________________

Additional Notes

8

Schools

When Texas wrote its new constitution at the end of the Civil War the government funded and ran all public schools. They did such a poor job with handling education that the people decided to create local school districts and fund these schools themselves. These Independent School Districts or ISD's swept across Texas and today the only state schools that exist are for the handicapped or college students.

The state accumulated a lot of money that was set aside for schools and they slowly started to funnel that money back into the ISDs with a few strings attached. Now we are right back to the state having more control, despite that the locals are still paying for the schools through their property taxes.

The state even came up with a way to make sure rich areas did not have nicer schools than poor areas. This was done by taking tax dollars from prosperous areas and giving it to poorer schools. Dubbed "The Robin Hood Plan" it stole from the rich and gave to the poor. At least we have truth in advertising, when they ignore the "ISD" on the side of school buses they are stealing from you.

So, what is the solution? I support vouchers and that might surprise many since we homeschooled both of our children. First, it's important to factor the amount each school receives per student. Then give a voucher worth 80% of that amount to the parents to spend on the education of their choice. These funds would be transferred at the end of each semester so that nobody can get paid and close shop, leaving the taxpayers holding the bill. Public schools would have smaller class sizes, more money per student and parents will have a choice where to send their kids.

We can pattern this after my VA benefits where the courts have already ruled, I can spend it where I wish be it a private, public or religious school because those are my benefits to spend as I wish, instead of tax money going to a church. Much like a government worker's pay being allowed to be donated to a church if they wish, your voucher could be used at a religious school with no constitutional issues.

Competition is only a first step; it will take concerned parents running and winning a majority of school board seats to curb the many issues the schools face. This is a great first step and it is doable with the right people serving.

What about homeschoolers? It might surprise you but homeschoolers are split about 50/50 on the voucher issue. Yes, they pay into the system and should receive these vouchers for educational expenses such as hiring a private tutor or curriculum. Concerns rise because many are fearful that eventually the money will have strings attached that would ruin the whole point of a truly "private" education. I can see their point and history is on their side. Which means any such program would need an opt out option. You have access to vouchers but if you don't want them, you are not forced to take them.

You can push your political party to adopt these vouchers as an issue. It's also easy enough to push candidates and officeholders to take a stand either for or against these vouchers.

Once "school choice" and competition is in the mix then we can address all the other issues. When you have the choice to take your children out of one school and place them elsewhere a lot of the issues will solve themselves.

Take Action

Step 1 Push your political party to adopt these vouchers as an issue. Ask candidates and officeholders to take a stand either for or against these vouchers.

Step 2 Competition in school board elections is done by getting parents involved to run and win these positions. These elections are nonpartisan, write down five possible candidates, approach each one and try to get them to run as a team.

Name____
Email/Phone____

Name____
Email/Phone____

Name____
Email/Phone____

Name____
Email/Phone____

Name____
Email/Phone____

Additional Notes

9

Executive Overreach State & Federal

I tell people all the time that not reading their national and state constitutions, "Bill of Rights," is akin to not reading the inventory when receiving an inheritance. If you have no idea what you have been given, how will you know when it has been stolen from you?

During 2020 the Texas "Republican" Governor gave delegated power he did not have to all County Judges that they had no right to wield. This was a clear violation of our state constitution and in some instances, the federal constitution.

Many media outlets and newspapers were more concerned with advertising dollars and getting interviews with the elected than actually reporting on the facts. If "Democracy Dies in the Dark" is the motto of those that report the news then they switched off the light, led it deep into the woods, shot it in the head and left it there. Over 300 days with the state of Texas being under "The Emergency Powers Act" an act that is, on its face, unconstitutional. It violates Article Two of the state constitution which lays out the separation of powers.

These delegated powers caused people across the state to be imprisoned without a crime, trial or conviction. Public beaches were closed when that is not allowed under the Texas Constitution. These powers also seized control of private businesses, closed churches and outlined which jobs were either "essential" or "non-essential." All of this at the whim of one man, Greg Abbott, with no one to appeal to because most courts were also shut down. I will call Abbott a dictator because the shoe fits and having seen what happened to people across Texas, I often drop the "tator."

The ONLY way to fix executive overreach is to replace the offenders, replace those who took an oath to defend us from them and refused. In Texas, the state legislators have the power to impeach an executive that practices such overreach and almost all of them failed to even try. I still run into state legislators such as Valorie Swanson that in an open meeting, stated she had no idea that the Texas House could call their own special session to consider impeachment. The power is granted under Texas Government Code 665.004. Either this multi-term state legislator is lying or really does not know how to protect us from executive overreach. Either option should disqualify her from holding public office.

To get rid of politicians it is often required to get the county parties from their district involved. In 2022 State Representative Chris Paddie was censured by three of the six counties he "represented" and the other three were looking at doing the same when he decided not to run for reelection and spend more time with his family.

Censure works, sometime even before the elections take place. The people in the party who do not like censure will tell everyone it means nothing. If censure doesn't hold any power, then why are they fighting so hard to keep it from happening?

If your county and state GOP refuses to hold the elected accountable then they need to be replaced. It all comes down to the precinct chairs, about 9,000 in Texas represent 254 counties. If you live elsewhere then your total will be much less and quicker to fill and replace. With the right people in these positions the County Chair becomes irrelevant. With the right people in those positions, the right delegates can be sent to the state convention and if they are, they can choose the right officers for the state party.

We cannot allow the elected executives to write, enforce and tell judges on how to rule on their whims that became law. This is not a limited, constitutional government and it is not a government based on separation of powers.

Take Action

Step 1 The ONLY way to fix executive overreach is to replace the offenders, replace those that took an oath to defend us and refused.

Step 2 To get rid of politicians it is often required to get the county parties from their district involved through a written censure. It works, sometime even before the next election takes place.

If your county and state GOP refuses to hold the elected accountable then they need to be replaced.

County Chair ________________________________
Email/Phone ________________________________

Precinct Chair ________________________________
Email/Phone ________________________________

SREC ________________________________
Email/Phone ________________________________

SREC_______________________________________
Email/Phone_________________________________

Party Vice Chair
Email/Phone_________________________________

Party Chairman______________________________
Email/Phone_________________________________

Additional Notes

____
____
____
____
____
____
____
____
____
____
____
____
____
____

10

Bureaucracy

In Washington D.C. and Alaska over 25% of the people work government jobs. Let that sink in for just a moment. That means every fourth person lives at the expense of the taxpayer before we even get to retirees or welfare recipients. Michigan and Indiana have the lowest number of government workers in the United States with just a tad over 10%. One in ten, are living at the expense of the other nine and again, this is not counting retirees nor welfare recipients. I will repeat, this 1 in 10 is the lowest ratio in the USA.

We simply cannot afford to support such a massive burden on the American taxpayer. The size and scope of government must be reduced. If that is not something a candidate or office holder will support and follow up on then they must be replaced before we fall as a nation.

We must start choosing representatives that will reduce the size of the government, not just slow the growth. If you have a tumor that will kill you past a certain point, would you pick a doctor who will remove it or one that will slow the growth? Too often we are forced to choose between two people who will increase the size and scope of government at almost identical rates. The only difference is that one will brag about how much faster they can make it grow while the other tells you they will make it grow slightly slower.

There are two kinds of spending in DC and in most state capitals. There are things that many of us depend on, such as military spending and that is too big to touch. Any congress member who wants to cut the military budget will be asked if they are willing to close the base in their district that would cost hundreds, if not thousands of jobs. If they are not willing then why would anyone else agree to reducing military spending? We spend roughly ten times as much as China, the next closest nation in terms of military spending.

Ask any veteran to tell you about the worst case of waste they ever saw while serving their country. Then ask if there were times when they did not have basic supplies. We could cut wasteful spending in half and use part of the savings for more bullets and toilet paper. We would have a stronger military than we have now and it would cost us only half as much. If we cannot keep up with China while spending five times as much, do you think spending ten times as much will matter?

There is a reason we don't all have bank vaults in our homes. At some point you can spend so much on defense you have nothing left to defend. We are reaching that point as a nation.

Take Action

Step 1 Start choosing representatives or find candidates that will reduce the size of the government, not just slow the growth. Track your current congress persons voting record on increased spending.

Congressional District_______________________________
Congress Person_____________________________________

Step 2 Find fiscal responsible conservatives who are willing to vote against waste and excessive spending. Write down five names of people you would like to see represent your district and reach out to them.

Name____
Email/Phone____

Name____
Email/Phone____

Name____
Email/Phone____

Name____
Email/Phone____

Name____
Email/Phone____

Additional Notes

____
____
____
____
____
____
____
____
____
____
____
____
____
____

11

Texit

Texit is specific to Texas and this is a separatist movement that believes becoming an independent nation again will solve a lot of issues for the state. There are groups in several states that advocate for independence and to become a separate nation. To be clear, I support holding the vote but I would advocate against the movement.

The idea of a socialist nation to the north and a failed drug state to the South is not a long-term positive solution for any nation. Without the Electoral College votes from Texas, I doubt any Republican would become president of the United States in my lifetime, if ever. As of this writing, Texas has 38 representatives in congress that would have to be reallocated based on population while in the Senate, Republicans would lose two more seats.

Even without those concerns, the state of Texas just re-elected a governor who violated the state constitution as many as 17 different ways during the Covid lockdowns. He also continues to renew his dictatorial "Emergency Powers" going on three years. If we cannot reform the state government we have and elect good people who will keep their oaths, how much worse will these people become when there is no federal government to which we can appeal out legal challenges?

How do we solve the issue with so many people wanting to separate from the United States? We fix the issues that are causing their dissatisfaction and we recruit these people to the task.

I believe the vote is destined to fail if it were to ever take place. Too many people in Texas depend on federal paychecks, federal contracts and US military bases to go along with Texit before we even factor in the other possible results of such a vote passing.

How do we get these people to help solve some actual issues? Agree to help them get the vote and point out that they will have to start replacing politicians and political party officers on both sides to push for that vote. Once they assist in filling these positions with good people many of the issues causing their dissatisfaction will get solved.

Point out that if we had real conservatives in the state and federal government, they would act less like our lord and masters. Electing good people would help make the nation look more like the Founders intended with the Feds handling only issues mentioned in the Constitution.

Why do career politicians choose to bow down to the federal government instead of standing up for the rights, that the people and the states have under our federal system? The answer is simple, they seek an even higher office. Almost every career politician wants the next higher office and once you are towards the top of the heap in state government then a federal position is the next logical step. The career politicians at the state level aspire to have all the power they can wield. They do this by abdicating more and more power to the federal government allowing them to create a career path. A path that allows them the possibility of more power in the future.

These careerists are too busy working on their next higher office or their reelection to their current office to do the job they currently have. The "swamp" is created by every one of these creatures by trading favors and support among each other to advance their careers at the expense of the nation.

Elect an actual person who believes in what the voters want, from either party, and watch how fast they get ridiculed and turned into memes. Conservative or liberal, if you fail to play the swamp games, expect to get belittled, criticized and marginalized until you go away. For those that refuse to go away, expect law enforcement to be called in to make your life a living hell. Even if the charges and the investigations yield nothing, the process can ruin you financially.

Expect anyone that obeys their oath to be belittled and made irrelevant by both sides. There are only two sides right now, life-long career politicians and the rest of us.

Take Action

Step 1 Recruit Texit people or other "single issue" groups to help them get their vote. This is a partnership; they would have to agree to help find new candidates in addition to replacing political party officers.

Additional Notes

____

____

____

____

____

12

Crime

How anyone needs to read the following is a mystery to me but here we go. If you do not allow the small stuff, you will end up with less of the big stuff. If you increase the penalty for future offenses, you will either frighten people straight or remove career criminals from the streets.

Rudy Giuliani was elected the mayor of New York because the system of ignoring petty crime escalated and resulted in more major crime. The American left laughed at the idea that severely punishing vandalism and shoplifting would do anything but clog up the system so that major crimes couldn't be handled. It turned out that the American left was wrong, once again.

By punishing the small infractions, the number of people graduating to more serious crimes were reduced and New York became safer. It became so safe that the voters thought they could once again elect Democrats to that position and look at the policies and crime rates now. The increased punishments for repeat offenders were lambasted by the left but the simple truth is that some people cannot be rehabilitated. At one point the FBI crime stats had the murder of police officers attributed to people with previous murder convictions at greater than 85%.

While I was working in Singapore, they had banners that read "Low crime does not mean no crime, please lock your doors." During the year I was visiting they had a total of 2,000 calls to the police stations across that nation. Now Singapore is a small place, only a couple of million people and 7 miles by 14 miles. People not only left their house and cars unlocked, they went on vacation for weeks or months without locking their doors. Many people in Singapore have no idea where their house keys are because they lost them years ago. That is how low crime is in that country.

You might be wondering, "Why are there so few criminals?" One reason is the sentencing. Say you stole a pack of smokes; the punishment might be three strokes with a cane or one year in prison. Ask yourself are you willing to have your ribs broken by being hit with a 20 ft.

long cane, soaked in water? Are you willing to have permanent scars from a split cane when it grabs your flesh and tears it when pulled back? A year in prison is no joke in Singapore; these are not pleasant places but I think I would choose the year.

Now say you get out of prison and decide to steal a car. Normally in this country that sort of crime would get you five years, with no possible parole option. I said normally but remember that year you served for the pack of smokes you stole? The judge will give you five years and then add on a year because you learned nothing from it the first time.

Let's say you get out again and steal another pack of smokes, the penalty increases to eight years. That is right, you get to reserve the first two sentences 1+6 and then another year for the smokes. If you fail to learn from 15 years in prison from the next pack of smokes you steal, it will cost you 16 years in prison. Do you see where career criminals do not last long in Singapore?

When I was working there on inflight entertainment systems, they caught a drug ring selling heroin. They were arrested on Monday and executed by hanging the following Friday. Yes, they have criminals, but not for long and not many.

We could realistically get rid of mandatory sentences for non-violent crimes and free up some prison space. Currently we are releasing violent offenders to make room for people that were caught attempting to sell a joint. Selling drugs carries a mandatory sentence but rape and murder do not? I have never done an illegal drug but as a father, husband, brother and son, can we keep the murderers and rapists off the streets even if it means releasing the drug vendors?

What can you do? Get involved in the various races for Judges and District Attorneys. Find out which ones are pushing "no bail and no jail" or are refusing to even file charges on theft of $1,000 or less, effectively decriminalizing theft below a certain level. These races are almost never high profile, nobody really brags about their favorite DA or Judge, but we should. We should care more about getting criminals off our streets than who sits in the oval office.

Take Action

Step 1 Get involved in the various primary election races for Judges and District Attorneys.

Judge____

Email/Phone____

DA____
Email/Phone_______________________________________

Additional Notes

13

Fake News

Where do we even start. At the time of this writing the Twitter files have been released showing the FBI paid millions to the Twitter platform, pushing them to suppress certain narratives and people. This is an easy one, the government is not allowed to censor private citizens nor are government agents. Pressuring a private company to do so does not make it constitutional.

The most concerning thing about this story is the response from the FBI itself that this was just "standard practice." Many thought this referred to social media but social media is just another form of "media" and what other media has the FBI been influencing, paying and pressuring to suppress our freedom of speech? This would explain why we have 50 news channels using the exact same wording in their reporting or the lack of coverage when certain politicians were targeted with protests.

The truth is that turning off the TV channel that lies to you and gets caught is the best solution. The right attempting to enforce "fairness" is no less destructive to free speech than the left setting up "disinformation boards."

Twitter was banning, shadow banning, blocking and choking down the reach of people sharing or attempting to share what turned out to be truth while amplifying the voices they agreed with or the FBI asked them to amplify. These same employees were leaving to work at the FBI and FBI agents were leaving to work for Twitter. Conservatives were leaving the platform and without the back-and-forth debate, liberals were leaving the echo chamber it was becoming. Imagine going into a gathering where everyone agreed with everything you said no matter what, how long would you stay and would you ever go back?

Fake news has always been with us and perhaps will always be with us but the best approach is to reward those that do it right and ignore into bankruptcy those that do it wrong. In the meantime, you can tear down their arguments to the bare bones and look for internal inconsistencies to their arguments and narratives. This does not take a degree or an above average intellect. You can do this with no special training. It just takes a bit of time and effort.

For example: "If NATO does not stop sending arms to Ukraine, Russia promises a large offensive." Sounds scary, but after ten months and 100K lost troops, was Russia really holding back this whole time? I recommend getting your news from a variety of sources, even reading or listening to the opposition sometimes gains you new insights. Even if you don't agree with them, at least you are better able to respond to their arguments if you take the time to compose such a response beforehand.

In our daily lives we must also recognize that our definition of words is not the same as what others mean when they use them. A good example of this is, "I am a great politician" to you this might mean they follow the constitution, the law and their oath. To a career politician it means they won reelection or an election to the next higher office. "I am an excellent attorney" to you that might mean they do their job quickly and defend the innocent. To some lawyers it means they maximize the number of hours they bill and get their clients, guilty or not, off the hook. Sometimes, if you ask, "What does that mean to you, explain your definition." They will answer honestly, to them it is self-evident that if they won the election, they were the better politician, not necessarily the better choice.

The other thing to watch out for is the "distraction" stories. Transexual issues affect a tiny fraction of a percent of people directly, a few hundred out of tens of millions. You must be able to rank the issues you care about in order of importance. With some things it is easy, breathing will always be more important than what flavor of ice cream you choose but in politics the minor issues can be made to overshadow the major or even underlying issues. "Beating the Democrats/Republicans" can make its way to the top of the priority list and push "Create a more perfect union" right off the charts.

Realize that both sides want what they think is best. Neither side wants only the right or left side of the road paved. Try and find common ground and build on those areas of agreement. You may never agree on tax issues but protecting children is as close to universal as it gets.

Take Action

Step 1 What are five issues you can agree one when talking to others.

#1 _____________________________________

____

____

#2 _____________________________________

____

____

#3 _____________________________________

____

____

#4 _____________________________________

____

____

#5 _____________________________________

____

____

14

Afterwards

What to say. First off, nothing in this book is my original idea or strategy. What you may have noticed is that every problem we have in this country has been caused by our government. All of which is fixable and I have compiled the best ideas, boiled them down in the most straightforward wording I could come up with. My focus was to make sure they met the "smell test" coming from a guy that has actually raised livestock.

What I put into this book is what I believe to be true. We may disagree on the strategy and timelines but if your goal is a better nation through conservative ideas, we can at least be uneasy allies. For those of you that believe in things that I do not, socialism for example or ignoring the 2nd Amendment then we are opponents, not enemies.

I will support and defend your right to make your arguments and to push your political beliefs, even as I seek to defeat you in the political realm. I know that in this increasingly divided political landscape that makes me a fool to some and a traitor to others but deal with it, to me it makes me an American.

The Founders gave us a great idea, generations have made it better and if we do our part there is no reason it cannot continue. It takes effort, it takes getting others involved and it will take action. A certain amount of notoriety might gain your message a larger audience but make sure the message and not the messenger is the focus.

It is my wish that people reading my books, watching my podcast or hearing me speak are inspired to do far more than what I have done. I wish to find the people to eclipse me, surpass me and to make my contributions irrelevant by comparison. I hope you are one of those people.

About Author

Robert West was born in Corpus Christi, Texas. Growing up in South and East Texas he enlisted in the Navy right out of high school. After six years in the service, he worked on aircraft electronics around the world for 30 years until turning to land development.

Robert met his wife, Carole, while stationed at Whidbey Island naval base. They have two adult children who are both veterans.

While being involved in his church and community for many years, The Five Star Plan began the first day of the Covid lockdowns in Texas. Since then, Robert has written, spoken and traveled across the state in an effort to return the government to the people and to end politics as a career choice.

THEFIVESTARPLAN.COM

"Career Politicians have caused all
our problems. Before fixing the problems,
eliminate the cause."

- Robert West

The Five Star Plan Reviews

The following reviews are from my first book. It's the citizens who must step up and take this country back.

Bob Hall, Texas Senator SD2

Robert West's book, "The Five Star Plan" lays out in clear, specific detail how "we the people" can regain our role in ensuring that our founding fathers' brilliant plan for life, liberty and individual pursuit of happiness can be rescued from the dominating hand of the socialist democrats who now control too many states and our nation. "The Five Star Plan" is a must read for every constitutional conservative with Judeo- Christian values.

Stephen Kallas, Collin County Precinct Chair

The Five Star Plan; Serves as a call to action with a good, workable plan that is showing results already; starting right in my home county. The book takes the idea that YOU can make a difference, providing a guide to how "we the people" can reassert our sovereignty. Therein the point-by-point explanation of the Constitutional violations was eye-opening and motivational at the same time. Read this book and get to work; your family, your church, your community and even Texas itself depends on your actions. It may just take our Lives, Fortunes, and Sacred Honor, if we don't act now.

Don Huffines, Huffines Liberty Foundation

"The Five Star Plan" is one of the most important books for Texas' future. Step by step, Robert West lays out how true patriots can and will take Texas back and ensure that Texas does not end up like so many other socialist democrat run cities and states. This book is a how-to manual for protecting and preserving the Constitution and our Founding Fathers' vision for America.

Rachal Hisler

The Five Star Plan is a book for everyone, whether you consider yourself to be political or not. Robert West has a real plan for real people to take our country back from the political machine that has become our ruling class. Every citizen must become engaged to ensure the God given rights to life, liberty, and the pursuit of happiness to our posterity. He includes simple, concise action items that are absolutely achievable no matter what area of The Lone Star State you call home.

Bryan Slaton, House Representative HD2

The Five Star Plan is a great resource for the nuts and bolts of Texas Politics from the ground up. In addition, also a great tool to help Republicans grow their support, educate their base and win new people to our cause.

Dan Thomas

In "The Five Star Plan" Robert West lays out a simple yet courageous vision of returning our government to citizen rule and ousting the career/profiteer politicians who lord over us like kings. This goal is attainable. "The Five Star Plan" is a great introduction to politics and how we got to this point. It's also a clear call to action for anyone ready to be a part of the solution.

Ed Wetterman

I got it on a Thursday about 4:30 and devoured it by 6:00 pm. The Five Star Plan is a way for us to take back our government. So, if you read this and agree, as I do, go find those five friends and get involved. It is not about winning for the Political Machine, it is about winning for the state of Texas, for doing what is right.

Mike Drury, Wise County Chair

The Five Star Plan is an inspiration for all Texans to realize that we the "normal" people have all the power to take back control of our great state. It has inspired me to get involved and help unite, educate and activate the people of Wise County. Robert lays it all out in simple easy to read terms. I would encourage anyone who is sick and tired of the status quo to quit watching the news, read the book and then get involved.

Aaron Sorrells

Robert West's book, "The Five Star Plan" is the perfect book to help every day Texans understand how they can be part of a bigger movement to replace out of touch and corrupt politicians. With his plan, we can put a stop to the political establishment that is destroying our way of life. It is a must read for everyone.

Elle Lark, Collin County Precinct Chair

I bought Robert's book as a brand-new precinct chair and after I heard him speak, I knew it was a worthy investment. Robert and his wife, Carole bring such knowledge and positive energy that is missing in today's political landscape. The information that Robert presents is empowering and inspiring. I highly recommend that anyone who cares about the future of Texas and our country go out of their way to read his book, hear him talk and meet him.

Chad Prather, Blaze Show Host

The Five Star Plan is a must read for anyone that cares about our future as Texans as well as the future of our nation. Now more than ever before we must mobilize to protect our freedom and our constitutional rights. The Five Star Plan will show you how to do that step-by-step.

Deanna Robertson, Harris County Precinct Chair

"Robert West's Five Star Plan spoke directly to my heart. For too long, we as Americans and Texans have been complacent; relying on and trusting that our elected officials were carrying out the things that we tasked them with. We are waking up and now living in the result of this complacency. The Five Star Plan lays out in clear detail how "we the people" can take back our government.

Tracy Jones

The Five Star Plan is a roadmap to the possible restoration of the Republican Party. A great vision for the future of the Republican Party is laid out in an easy-to-understand manner. The Five Star Plan is an excellent read.

Stormy Bradley

Robert West's book, "The Five Star Plan" is a clear roadmap for regular people and groups that are focused on putting Texas voters back in charge and replacing career politicians with patriots. It outlines where to be active and how to make a positive impact in local and state government. It is an actionable and practical plan for regular people who want to unite and protect our liberties in Texas. It is a must read for all Texas Conservatives that are tired of the stagnation.

Andy Hopper

The Five Star Plan has been an instrumental tool to the conservative group I helped found, Wise County Conservatives. WCC helped activate Republican voters in the county and, with the guidance of Robert West, helped our GOP fill empty precinct seats. This change was desperately needed as our county has been redistricted into a more moderate district and the county Republican Party will need to be fully functional and strong to maintain Republican wins. Now, as a candidate, I also appreciate the functional nature of The Five Star Plan in getting out the vote. I expect our county's voter turnout to be higher than ever before.

Greg Caldwell

The Five Star Plan lays out, in easy steps, how an ordinary citizen can help take back our country. In layman's terms, it is a "how-to manual" for returning our country back to our founding beliefs. If you want to help save our country, this book should be on your short list for must read books.

John McIntyre

Excellent analysis and wealth of information on getting involved and making a difference!

Jim Herblin

Frustrated conservatives want to know what they can do to help save our states and nation. The five-star plan is a straightforward way to get conservatives on the "political field" to effectuate and reinstate Constitutional principles and Christian values.

Kim Spain

I just finished his book last night. It's an easy read and put things in a way that empowers the average person. It gives basic info for the newbie without making us who know more feel like we are wasting our time. All around awesome book.

Joe McDaniel

When I finished reading the 5 Star Plan, I immediately had to call Robert West. It was, as if, I had read a book about myself. What has birthed in Robert is what is being birthed into a movement. We are sick and tired of the career establishment running the political arena. Politicians have got to go! We can elect Patriots! What has happened to the idea of "We the People"? It is all about freedom, liberty, and the pursuit of happiness. Stop those from taking that away from us. Join forces and train 5 to reach 5 that can train 5 to reach 5 more. Get involved in both small and big ways. Constitutional Conservatives can take back this country one vote at a time.

George Lavender

Robert West's Five Star Plan couldn't have come at a better time. Over the past few years, we have seen the damage that has been done by lawmakers that we trusted to be conservative. Whether it's at the state or Federal level, many have shown that they do not share our values. The Five Star Plan lays out a roadmap to take our government back. Robert gives us hope that we can change things for the better.

Jen Benzer

The Five Star plan was an excellent roadmap on how to change the "old-school" political system. It gave me great hope as a 1st-time candidate for State office. This book takes complex issues and provides constitutional solutions; the Five Star Plan is a must-read for all new candidates

Mike Monreal

"Clear, Concise, Compelling. The Five Star Plan charts the course for conservatives to take back our Texas grassroots, conservative values. Robert West's stories, facts and practical steps will help conservatives align and create the momentum needed to replace career politicians with Patriot Citizen-Legislators."

Gayle Summers

I thoroughly enjoyed reading Mr. West's book and I highly recommend it to any true Texan that is serious about saving our great state. I will always remember, I am (the) public, and those I elect are public servants.

Bob Brewer, Smith County Precinct Chair

The Five Star Plan is the Mother Lode at Sutter's Mill. Every sentence is a gold nugget of priceless information. It's The concise action plan to retrieve our counties, state, and nation from those who think they own the world. When you're in a group that thinks "doing something" is designing a tee shirt logo, or recruiting a speaker, give them this book and require a written report by next meeting. This PLAN will "get er done"! Read it, adsorb it, execute it, recruit, and pray. God will smile on you as He smiled on Robert when He had him write this book for you and our progeny. God Bless Robert West

Jo Holland

Bless you Robert for bringing patriots together. Texas is being Invaded by liberal Democrats and illegals and Dems say boldly they want to turn our state Blue! GOD forbid! I'm 84 and can't do the active things anymore BUT my spirit is strong, and I want to see your 5-star plan succeed.

David Lowe

The Five Star Plan is not just any book. Reading it is an experience and the amount of information covered in this very easy read is extraordinary. Anyone who has ever considered getting involved in politics, the Five Star Plan is a great first step.

Chad Miller

As a lifelong businessman who has never run for office, The Five Star Plan has been an invaluable resource for me in my campaign for County Judge in Wise County. The priority list is rock solid and an easy for any actual conservative to get behind and the different reference points in the book are informative, concise, and something each Patriot in Texas should be aware of. I know Robert and Carole personally and their character is a testimony to how effective the plan is. I highly recommend anyone getting into politics or even a seasoned vet to get behind The Five Star Plan.

Jonathan Hullihan

The "The Five Star Plan" is a definitive pathway toward empowering the grassroots, to take back the power of the people from those who would misuse it for personal agendas, counter to the will of the people, under the guise of public service.

Shelley Luther

The Five Star Plan by Robert West is the quintessential "How to" for citizens who are ready to take their first steps toward political action. This book maps the political course for anyone who's fed up with the current status of our nation, state and local governments and has the desire to implement change. No stone is left unturned and excuses of political ignorance are extinguished. This is a must read for new and veteran activists.

Larry Dale Carpenter

"Absolutely loved The Five Star Plan! This is a must read for anyone new or seasoned to politics. It outlines the pure patriotic duties that we need to take if we want to take back our state and country. The Bible, USA Constitution and The Five Star Plan are the most important reads."

Julia Schmoker

When I read The Five Star Plan it was like looking in a mirror. I am precisely who this book is for and about. Patriots not Politicians. We need patriots to protect the constitution so our rights are never violated again. Shutting down the economy, schools and houses of worship is unconstitutional. Mandates, vaccinations and vaccine passports are all infringing on our freedom. We need fresh representatives and strict adherence to the constitution to right this ship. The tenets of The Five Star Plan is the way to secure our freedom.

Dennis London

The Five Star Plan is exactly what it says it is – a plan to replace Politicians with Patriots. It is probably one of the most important books for the future of Texas. Robert West clearly defines and lays out how true patriots can take Texas back and ensure this great state does not end up like the democrat-run cities and states. If you are a Constitutional Conservative with Judeo- Christian values, and you find yourself wondering how a Texas House and Senate with a Republican majority still can't get traction on important issues – and more importantly, if you want to do something about it - then this book is an absolute must-read! Don't sit on the sidelines. If you want something different to happen, then you need to do things differently.

Isaac Smith

"The Five Star Plan is the road map leading to the political trenches. If you want to save our country, if you want to move past voting & want to get involved then this is your book! Our country is worth our fight, our efforts & our time. The Five Star Plan will give you the direction & insight into how we do this together!"

Carol Montgomery

I attended your class months ago and because of you and your book I am now the Precinct Chair Thank you for all that you do. Your class was what I needed to move forward and now the real work begins! Warm Regards.

Blake West

This isn't a typical motivation book that tells you how you should feel and make yourself feel good while doing nothing. This is a book that anyone can use to help make a difference so long as the reader is willing to put in the work. Most questions people ask, will be answered. It's up to every Texan to step up now. Do everything we can peacefully before we consider the long-term bloodshed. If we don't history will remember us as the generation that threw Texas in the dumpster. I don't know about you but if future generations ask, "Why did we do nothing to preserve our Liberty?" My response will be, "People never knew how good they had it until it was too late. They didn't do enough in the development towards raising their children because it was easier for the government to do it for them." They were ultimately too lazy because they never cared about future generations, only themselves. I however will not be one of those selfish sheep. "I won't stop fighting until I die or restore our freedoms we once had."

Jennifer Yoch

This book contains how to become better informed about Texas politics. What to consider if running for election. How to create a network to elect conservatives for 2022. 10 priorities for the Texas legislative agenda and a summary of what our elected officials do. I think this will become a guide map for those of us seeking to get more involved. Thanks for writing this great book!

Charity Leitz

This is a book based on the political climate in Texas, but the information and suggestions detailed in the text are applicable in any state. It's a MUST read for any patriot who is tired of the dictator like politicians and the lack of accountability for those running our country. If you're looking to help, make a change happen- GET THIS BOOK.

Ricky Williams

A fellow Patriot suggested we read Robert West's book, The Five Star Plan. This book absolutely spoke to us and to what was stirring in our hearts. While the book is targeted to Texas, the message translates to any state and this country needs a reboot of freedom-loving, Constitutional Conservatives taking a stand. We need to get back to center and if you love this country, I urge you to join us in replacing Politicians with Patriots. We will need all hands-on deck as we take on big money politicians and opportunists alike. We hope that you'll lock arms and join our efforts.

Art Hernandez

"For too long, the majority has been silent. The Five Star Plan by Robert West gives the silent majority the guidance to take back America."

Tracy Lasater

Robert West showed up early and matched our group perfectly. He truly exceeded our expectation, and we will be inviting him back to speak with our group. Thank you so much for coming to Nacogdoches Conservative Watch.

Dewey Collier

Robert West's "The Five Star Plan" provides the reader a look into the Texas political establishment. He points out how the current RINO's who are in the Texas legislature have violated their oath to God, Texas Constitution, and their constituents. The plan provides a step-by-step outline of techniques that every individual running or wanting to run for public office could adopt. I especially found the idea of growing your campaign though a five supporters pyramid model to be personally motivating. The Five Star Plan helps to strengthen Texas by advancing the Republican Platform, fighting to maintain Texan values, independence, entrepreneurship and freedom.

Beverly Rachel

I've heard you speak at our Patriot meeting, and I read your blog but... Your Book... Just WOW! Thank you for writing this!

Sandra Pierce

I am so proud of you both. I know what others do not see. Carole helps my brother so much; through encouraging him and him for you. Y'all are a great team! I pray for you both and this mission that you are on, it is for now and for the future of our next generation. I know that our families before us fought for our country and her freedoms. I pray that 50 years from now that someone will mention you both in their prayers, thanking God for what you both accomplished and knowing you both were family who loved and fought for our country.

Casey Sollock

Robert West is amazing! He recently spoke at our Saving Texas event in Austin. He is personable, kind, positive, and humble, and his message is SPOT ON. I really appreciated his insight into the mess we find ourselves in surrounding Texas politics, and I especially appreciated his Five Star Plan solution! Thank goodness he has a Plan. Not only is his Plan SPOT ON, he conveys his message with passion, resilience, and confidence. While one could look at the current political landscape and feel despair, Robert empowers us with an actionable plan which brings hope. We can't wait to have him back again! I highly recommend Robert as a speaker, and I wholeheartedly endorse his Five Star Plan. This is the Plan that will save Texas.

Erika Hatfield, Convention of States Coordinator

As the State Grassroots Coordinator for the Convention of States in Texas, I'm always trying to find more information to share with others on the inside scoop of Texas civics and how to strategically take our state and country back from tyranny. The government, regardless at what level, was never meant to have so many tentacles reaching into the depths of our lives. This book explains the meaning of self-governance and the steps we need to take as citizens to release the choke hold the government has on our lives.

Kasey Britton

Robert West is a precinct chair in my county. God crossed our paths during my mayoral campaign. After chatting with he and his sweet wife, Carole, I learned he wrote a book, The Five Star Plan. Being a newbie to politics, I purchased the book and read it in one day! From that point on, I knew this was exactly what I was looking for. When I began my political journey a year ago, I knew connecting information to voters was absolutely necessary! Being new to politics and finding info was hard and when asking questions with seasoned political folks, it was always met with feeling like I was crazy for asking. Robert's book solved this problem. He and Carole are true Patriots and helping folks like me get information into the hands everyone in this state. The Five Star Plan is the only plan everyone should get behind.

Rick Parent

Robert West's "The Five Star Plan" is a well written, well laid out "How To" Book. It tells you what it's going to tell you, then tells you and reiterates the points covered in every chapter! It's a very well laid out plan for opening eyes before we proceed any further on the insane political path, we find ourselves. Make no mistake about it this NOT another rant and it is NOT another diatribe that bolsters your opinions. It IS a personal challenge to all of us to make a difference in the history books. A very stimulating read that moves at the speed of cliff notes! While he never takes you out of your comfort zone, Robert gives us a road map to breaking our personal best efforts correcting the problems that have infected our political world.

Brett Guilory

In a time period of deep frustration with establishment politicians, candidates, and their policies, "The Five Star Plan" is a fantastic guide for Texans on how we can replace these establishment personalities with hardworking Americans that truly represent The People. The book is a call-to-arms for anyone who is looking to get involved, make a difference, and become a part of the movement that truly protects our liberties and freedoms and preserves the Constitution and our American way of life.

Bianca Garcia

We the people have to light up a grassroot movement like never before this election cycle. We must elect patriots who will actually pass a term limit bill, eliminate the emergency powers of the Governor, end property taxes, and deliver on school choice once and for all. I recommend Robert West's book especially for those who are new to the political process. "The Five Star Plan" should be in every patriot's home and reading list to remind us that WE HOLD the POWER! Thank You Robert for what you are doing! Let's win and take back Texas!

George Tyson

In today's government career and corrupt politicians are so entrenched that it is hard to remove them from office even with an energized populace. By using Robert West's, The Five Star Plan as the blue print, true patriots can take back their government and return it to "For the People". The Five Star Plan was originally written for Texas politics but it can be used anywhere and at any level of government. Patriots who are new to politics can start locally with School Boards, City Councils and County governance or take the plunge and go after State or National office. As long as the plan is followed any elected office is available to patriots. The why is in your heart, the how has been given to you by Robert West, now is the time to put the plan into action and regain our country.

Dan Johnson

America today is in a crisis that has not been seen since the Civil War. About half the leadership of the country no longer have any respect for the US Constitution when it doesn't fit their agenda. A representative republic can only survive if a majority of the people want it to. Texas has long been looked at as an example of freedom thinkers and patriots to the rest of America. But even Texas is sliding away. This book points out how even Conservative Republicans like Greg Abbott and the Texas Legislature have ignored the Texas State Constitution. If we allow this type of leadership to continue, Texas and America, is doomed to the complete loss of individual liberty. But what separates this book from many others is it doesn't just show a problem, it offers an Idea, A Plan, to fix things. It just takes a little effort, from everyone, who believes in and wants their children to live in the "Land of the free and the home of the Brave" instead of the Land of the regulated and the home of the compliant. Just casting your vote isn't enough anymore to fix what is broken with Texas, or America.

Tim Labatsky

Picked up the book after hearing him speak at a Patriot Owned Business event. This is a must read for any Patriot that loves this country and asks, "what can I do?" You can see his passion thru the pages of this book. All I can say is pick one up and find out for yourself.

Joshua Hamm

While talking with the Madison County GOP I was asked an important question, "How can we trust you to do what you're running on?" The short answer, you can't. The long answer is that The Five Star Plan shows how politicians can be held accountable to their constituents. Counties have the power to publicly censure civil servants and expose individuals who are not holding up their side of the bargain. All politicians are dependent upon donations from individuals and organizations to run campaigns, it is much more difficult to raise money if they are publicly ostracized by their own party. Conservatives must remove the beam from our own eye before anything else.

Bob Steinhagen, Bunker Bob Show

Apathy & indifference are the single greatest threat to American liberty and The Five Star Plan is a practical handbook for fed-up patriots who are ready to act. Those who brandish the conservative moniker are challenged by it to stand on principle over loyalty to a Party that continues to stand up for politicians whose actions betray some of the most foundational standards of its platform. Because of its brevity and large print, one might presume that it's an easy read, however, there is nothing easy about learning how to peacefully and patriotically take action against the swamp-mentality of the established GOP by standing on the conviction of one's belief.

Amanda L'Esperance, Delta County Precinct Chair

Buy the book, drain the swamp and take back the power of the people. Robert West has put it in plain English.

Mark Middleton

For years Liberal-Democrats have had and implemented a "plan" to take over Texas. Thanks to Robert West, we Conservatives now have a plan to take Texas back from the Socialists. In the 'Five Star Plan' Robert lays out a succinct road map we Conservatives can employ to ensure Texas is restored to its rightful place as the Conservative leader in the Union. For years, Texas has been controlled by Establishment politicians, the sub-title of his book is "Replacing Politicians with Patriots," if Texans will follow the "Five Star Plan" that's what we will do.

Adrienne Balkum

Robert West gives an easy-to-read approach on how people can take simple steps to get involved right in your own community. From the beginning he educates you so that you are informed of what was violated by Governor Greg Abbott from our supreme law of the land the Constitution. This book provides insight on commitments, recruiting volunteers, campaign team member ideas and an overview how to analyze voter rolls.

Jonathan Mitchell

The Five Star plan by Robert West is an excellent guide on how we can restore our constitutional rights by electing candidates and having everyday common folks run for public office that will stand by our core principles. This guide will also help out on the federal level by ensuring our US Representatives for Texas stands by the constitution and ensure that the states have the power over the federal government and stopping the federal over-reach.

Elizabeth Norris

It's time for Americans to take our country back. The Five Star Plan is an excellent resource on how we as Americans can start that process! What a great educational tool for all.

Lee Finley

Robert West's "The Five Star Plan" is, at its core, a roadmap. West reveals a path by which the reader can make a real, positive impact on the world around them, starting at the local level. He demonstrates how we can remove corrupt, self-serving, lifetime politicians, and replace them with Citizen Leaders committed to the principles of full transparency, integrity, and limited Government. "The Five Star Plan" is less a defense of Conservative Republican values, and more a step-by-step guide to accomplishing real, tangible, political change. Read it. Absorb it. Act on it.

Erleigh Wiley, Kaufman County DA

Texas is the greatest state in our union, but to keep our great state for future generations, it is imperative that we have a government that serves the people and not special interests. West's book sets out a roadmap for the citizens of Texas: get involved in the electoral process, hold your elected officials accountable, and ensure conservatives of conviction have control of our state government. The Five Star Plan is a straight forward "how to" book. Every officeholder and those interested in holding office should take the time to read.

Warren Wade

"This book is a great primer for the important issues of the day with practical advice on how to address those issues. Highly recommended!"

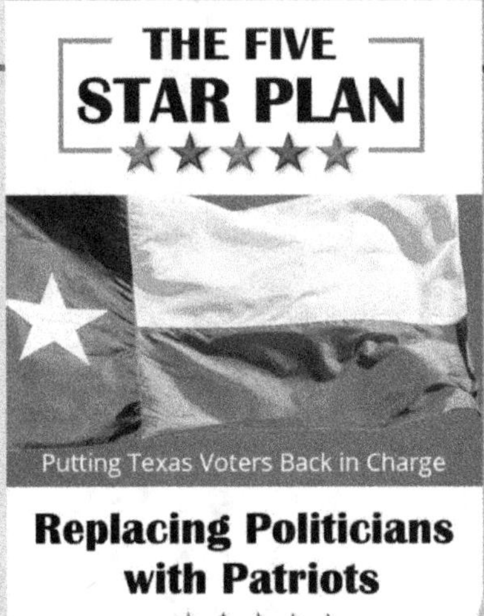

A REAL PLAN
THAT WORKS
THE FIVE
STAR PLAN
Putting Texas Voters Back in Charge
Replacing Politicians
with Patriots
ROBERT WEST
GET
STARTED
TODAY
ROBERT
WEST
PODCAST
YOUTUBE & RUMBLE
THEFIVESTARPLAN.COM